# The Cabbage

# Patch Cookbook

Healthy, Delicious and Simple Cabbage Recipes

## BY: Nancy Silverman

# COPYRIGHT NOTICES

||||||||||||||||||||||||||||||||||||||||||||||||||||||||||||||||||||||||||||

# My Heartfelt Thanks and A Special Reward for Your Purchase!

*https://nancy.gr8.com*

My heartfelt thanks at purchasing my book and I hope you enjoy it! As a special bonus, you will now be eligible to receive books absolutely free on a weekly basis! Get started by entering your email address in the box above to subscribe. A notification will be emailed to you of my free promotions, no purchase necessary! With little effort, you will be eligible for free and discounted books daily. In addition to this amazing gift, a reminder will be sent 1-2 days before the offer expires to remind you not to miss out. Enter now to start enjoying this special offer!

||||||||||||||||||||||||||||||||||||||||||||||||||||||||||||||||||||||||||||||

# Table of Contents

Chapter I - Cabbage Salad Recipes ......................................... 7

(1) Coleslaw of All Colors..................................................... 8

(2) Coleslaw and Beef Baps.................................................. 11

(3) Red Pepper Coleslaw ..................................................... 14

(4) Delicious and Simple Coleslaw...................................... 16

(5) Ruby Red Coleslaw ...................................................... 18

(6) Crunchy Nut Coleslaw .................................................. 20

(7) Tangy Lemon Slaw........................................................ 22

(8) Creamy Coleslaw Salad ................................................. 24

(9) Appetizing Apple Coleslaw ........................................... 26

(10) Scrumptious Fruity Coleslaw....................................... 28

Chapter II - Cabbage Soup Recipes....................................... 30

(11) Cabbage and Beetroot Soup.......................................... 31

(12) Irish Cabbage and Bacon Soup ..................................... 35

(13) Ham and Cabbage Soup ................................. 37

(14) Cabbage, Carrot and Potato Soup................................ 39

(15) Cabbage and Tomato Soup ........................................ 41

(16) Simple Cabbage Soup ................................. 43

(17) Slow Cooker Cabbage and Cannellini Bean Soup........ 46

(18) Beef Cabbage Soup.................................... 48

(19) Winter Spicy Cabbage Soup ........................ 51

(20) Russian Cabbage Soup ............................... 54

Chapter III - Assortment of Cabbage Recipes ......................... 57

(21) Cabbage Pancakes ..................................... 58

(22) Cabbage and Onion Mixture ....................................... 61

(23) Barbecued Cabbage .................................... 64

(24) Cabbage Tofu Noodles Mix ....................................... 66

(25) Braised Cabbage........................................ 69

(26) Beef, Cabbage and Mushroom Noodles...................... 71

(27) Potato and Cabbage Sauté .......................... 74

(28) Vegetable Noodles ..................................................... 76

(29) Pork Oriental Cabbage Rolls ....................................... 79

(30) Stuffed Cabbage Rolls ................................................ 82

About the Author .................................................................. 86

Author's Afterthoughts ........................................................ 88

# Chapter I – Cabbage Salad Recipes

||||||||||||||||||||||||||||||||||||||||||||||||||||||||||||||||||||||||||||||||||||

# (1) Coleslaw of All Colors

A nutritious, raw and fresh delicious coleslaw made from spring onions, carrots, kale, parsley, white and red cabbage.

**Prep Time:** 15 **minutes**

**Yield:** 4 **people**

**Total Calories:** 34

## Ingredient List:

- ½ a red cabbage, finely chopped
- ½ a white cabbage, finely chopped
- 2 bunches of parsley, finely chopped
- 1 bunch of kale, finely chopped
- 4 carrots, finely chopped
- 12 spring onions, finely chopped

## Ingredient for The Dressing

- 250 milliliters of olive oil, extra virgin and cold pressed
- 65 grams of raw cashews (soaked for 4 hours)
- The juice of one lemon wedge
- 4 cloves of crushed garlic
- A pinch of sea salt

|||||||||||||||||||||||||||||||||||||||||||||||||||||||||||||||||||||||||||

**Instructions:**

1. Combine the vegetables together in a large bowl.
2. combine the ingredients for the dressing in a food processor.
3. Pour the dressing over the vegetables and stir together thoroughly.
4. Place in the refrigerator until you are ready to serve.

# (2) Coleslaw and Beef Baps

Red cabbage and beetroot coleslaw brings some lively texture and color into this delicious lean roast beef bap.

**Prep Time:** 10 **minutes**

**Yield:** 4 **people**

**Total Calories:** 78

**Ingredient List:**

- 4 Tbsp. of mayonnaise, reduced fat
- 4 tsp. of wholegrain mustard
- 4 whole meal large baps
- 50 grams of watercress
- 300 grams of thinly sliced roast beef
- 200 grams of finely shredded red cabbage
- 1 finely sliced red cabbage
- 1 finely sliced red onion
- 150 grams of peeled cooked beetroot coarsely grated
- 6 Tbsp. of natural yoghurt, low-fat

||||||||||||||||||||||||||||||||||||||||||||||||||||||||||||||||||||||||||||||

**Instructions:**

1. Combine the mustard and mayonnaise in large bowl and whisk together thoroughly.

2. Spread the top and the bottom half of the baps with the mixture.

3. Top the baps with the roast beef and the water cress.

4. In the same large bowl add the beetroot, red onion, and the red cabbage. Add the yogurt and stir to coat.

5. Spoon the coleslaw on top of the beef baps, season with pepper, put the baps together and serve.

# (3) Red Pepper Coleslaw

An exotic Latin styled coleslaw embellished with olive oil and lemon.

**Prep Time:** 15 **minutes**

**Yield:** 12 **people**

**Total Calories:** 43

## Ingredient List:

- 1 bunch of fresh coriander
- 1 red pepper
- 7 Tbsp. of extra virgin olive oil
- The juice of 4 lemons
- 1 dash of salt
- 1 large shredded cabbage head
- 2 small chopped tomatoes

||||||||||||||||||||||||||||||||||||||||||||||||||||||||||||||||||||||||||

## Instructions:

1. Place the red pepper, coriander, lemon juice and olive oil into a food processor until the pepper and the coriander are finely chopped.
2. Add the cabbage and tomatoes into a large bowl, coat with the coriander mixture and stir together thoroughly.
3. Place in the fridge until you are ready to serve.

# (4) Delicious and Simple Coleslaw

Homemade coleslaw will always be the best! This is a simple recipe made with mayonnaise, cabbage, red onions and carrots.

**Prep Time:** 20 **minutes**

**Yield:** 8 **people**

**Total Calories:** 35

## Ingredient List:

- 3 medium grated carrots
- 1 grated red onion
- ½ a grated white cabbage
- 3 Tbsp. of mayonnaise
- 1 tsp. of lemon zest
- Basil leaves
- Lemon Zest

||||||||||||||||||||||||||||||||||||||||||||||||||||||||||||||||||||||||||

## Instructions:

1. In a large bowl, combine the cabbage, onions and carrots. Add the mayonnaise and stir together thoroughly.
2. Add the salt, pepper, lemon zest and a few torn pieces of basil leaves.

# (5) Ruby Red Coleslaw

Delicious, fresh, crunchy coleslaw made with red pepper, red onion, carrot and red cabbage, doused in a creamy dressing.

**Prep Time:** 10 **minutes**

**Yield:** 4 **servings**

**Total Calories:** 28

## Ingredient List:

- ¼ finely sliced red cabbage
- ½ a grated carrot
- ½ a red onion, thinly sliced
- ½ a finely sliced red onion
- 3 Tbsp. of mayonnaise
- 4 Tbsp. of light salad cream
- 3 tsp. of caster sugar
- Salt and pepper to taste
- 2 Tbsp. of rice vinegar

IIIIIIIIIIIIIIIIIIIIIIIIIIIIIIIIIIIIIIIIIIIIIIIIIIIIIIIIIIIIIIIIIIIIIII

## Instructions:

1. Combine the vegetables in a large mixing bowl.
2. In a small bowl, combine the rice vinegar, salt and pepper, caster sugar, salad cream and mayonnaise, stir together thoroughly.
3. Pour the dressing over the vegetables and stir together thoroughly.
4. Place in the fridge until you are ready to serve.

# (6) Crunchy Nut Coleslaw

A unique coleslaw recipe made with roasted peanuts, sweet sultanas, spring onions, radishes, and white cabbage.

**Prep Time:** 15 **minutes**

**Yield:** 4 **people**

**Total Calories:** 49

## Ingredient List:

- 200 grams of finely shredded white cabbage
- 1 coarsely grated large carrot
- 50 grams of sultanas
- 4 finely chopped spring onions with the green and white parts separated
- 2 Tbsp. of mayonnaise
- 150 grams of low-fat plain yogurt
- 30 grams of sliced radishes
- 50 grams of roasted peanuts, unsalted
- 3 Tbsp. of chopped parsley
- Salt and pepper

IIIIIIIIIIIIIIIIIIIIIIIIIIIIIIIIIIIIIIIIIIIIIIIIIIIIIIIIIIIIIIIIIIIIIIIIIIIIIIIIIIII

## Instructions:

1. In a large bowl, mix the white part of the spring onions, sultanas, carrot and cabbage.
2. In a small bowl, combine the yogurt and the mayonnaise and season with pepper and salt.
3. Add the dressing to the cabbage and toss to coat the ingredients.
4. Add the peanuts and radishes, sprinkle with the parsley and the green part of the spring onions.

# (7) Tangy Lemon Slaw

A simple and delicious tangy addition to any BBQ or salad, made with radishes, red onions, carrots and cabbage.

**Prep Time:** 20 **minutes**

**Yield:** 4 **people**

**Total Calories:** 34

## Ingredient List:

- ¼ white thinly shredded cabbage
- 1 medium grated carrot
- ½ a red onion finely chopped
- 3 radishes finely chopped
- 3 Tbsp. of mayonnaise
- The juice and zest of half a lemon
- Salt and black pepper

||||||||||||||||||||||||||||||||||||||||||||||||||||||||||||||||||||||||||||

## Instructions:

1. Combine all the ingredients in a medium sized bowl, and combine together thoroughly.
2. Place in the fridge until you are ready to serve.

# (8) Creamy Coleslaw Salad

Delicious creamy coleslaw adorned with tomato and cucumber.

**Prep Time:** 20 **minutes**

**Yield:** 4 **people**

**Total Calories:** 33

**Ingredient List:**

- 375 grams of chopped cabbage
- 1 chopped tomato
- ½ a chopped cucumber
- ½ a chopped red onion
- 1 Tbsp. of sugar
- 1 tsp. of salt
- ½ a tsp. of ground black pepper
- 1 Tbsp. of mayonnaise

||||||||||||||||||||||||||||||||||||||||||||||||||||||||||||||||||||||||||||||

**Instructions:**

1. Put all the ingredients into a large bowl and stir thoroughly to combine.

# (9) Appetizing Apple Coleslaw

A refreshing combination of fruits and vegetables to make this delicious apple coleslaw.

**Prep Time:** 15 **minutes**

**Yield:** 4 **people**

**Total Calories:** 56

## Ingredient List:

- 1 bag of coleslaw mix
- 2 sliced apples
- 2 sticks of sliced celery
- 4 Tbsp. of vegetable oil
- 2 Tbsp. of lemon juice
- 2 Tbsp. of honey

||||||||||||||||||||||||||||||||||||||||||||||||||||||||||||||||||||||||||||

## Instructions:

1. In a medium sized bowl, combine the coleslaw mix, celery, apples and mix together thoroughly.
2. In another medium sized bowl, mix together the honey, lemon and the oil then pour mixture over the coleslaw. Mix together thoroughly to combine.
3. Place in the refrigerator until you are ready to serve.

# (10) Scrumptious Fruity Coleslaw

A delectable combination of cabbage, carrots, mayonnaise, natural yogurt and raisins. This makes a great side dish for burgers, quiche or salad.

**Prep Time:** 10 **minutes**

**Yield:** 6 **people**

**Total Calories:** 37

## Ingredient List:

- 300 grams of finely shredded cabbage
- 200 grams of grated cabbage
- 40 grams of raisins
- 2 Tbsp. of mayonnaise
- 200 grams of plain yogurt
- Salt and pepper

||||||||||||||||||||||||||||||||||||||||||||||||||||||||||||||||||||||||||||

## Instructions:

2. In a large bowl, add the raisins, carrots and cabbage and stir together thoroughly.
3. In a small bowl, combine the yoghurt, mayonnaise, salt and pepper and stir together thoroughly.
4. Pour the sauce over the vegetables and stir together thoroughly.
5. Place in the fridge until you are ready to serve.

# Chapter II - Cabbage Soup Recipes

||||||||||||||||||||||||||||||||||||||||||||||||||||||||||||||||||||||||||||

# (11) Cabbage and Beetroot Soup

A tasty vegetarian soup made by with a combination of kidney beans, potatoes, celery, carrots, mushrooms, cabbage and beetroot.

**Prep Time:** 20 **minutes**

**Total Prep Time:** 1 **hour**

**Yield:** 8 **people**

**Total Calories:** 76

**Ingredient List:**

- 1 liter of water
- 2 trimmed and washed beetroots
- 675 grams of chopped tomatoes
- 115 grams of tomato puree
- 30 grams of butter
- 2 chopped red onions
- 140 grams of chopped mushrooms
- 2 chopped carrots
- 2 chopped celery sticks
- 4 Tbsp. of fresh dill, chopped and divided
- 1 vegetable stock cube
- 2 large cubed white potatoes
- ½ a head of chopped green cabbage
- The juice of 1 lemon
- Salt and pepper
- 250 millilitres of soured cream

**Instructions:**

1. Put the beetroots into a large saucepan and pour 1 litre of water over the top. Increase the heat to the highest temperature and bring it to a boil.

2. Turn the heat to low, place a lid over the saucepan and simmer for 40 minutes.

3. Place the tomato puree and the tomatoes into a food processor, blend and set it to one side.

4. Heat the butter in a frying pan over medium heat. Add the onions and cook for approximately 5 minutes until they become translucent.

5. Add the mushrooms and cook for another 10 minutes.

6. Add the vegetable stock, half of the dill, tomato mixture, celery and carrots, stir to combine and cook for a further 10 minutes.

7. Use a slotted spoon to remove the beetroot, transfer them into a bowl and place them in the freezer.

8. Add the water, kidney beans and the liquid, potatoes, and the mushroom mixture into the beetroot water. Bring it to a boil over medium heat, turn the heat down to low put a lid on the saucepan and cook for a further 20 minutes.

9. Peel the beetroots and then grate them, add the cabbage, beetroot and remaining dill into the saucepan. Put the lid back on it and continue to simmer for a further 5 minutes.

10. Season with the salt and pepper and add the lemon juice.

11. Take the soup off the cooker; let it rest for a minimum of 2 hours.

12. Bring it to a boil again, spoon out into bowls and serve with soured cream.

# (12) Irish Cabbage and Bacon Soup

This is a fantastic simple and chunky soup. The cherry red color of the tomatoes and the dark green cabbage make for a beautiful palette of colors in your bowl.

**Prep Time:** 15 **minutes**

**Total Prep Time:** 30 **minutes**

**Yield:** 4 **people**

**Total Calories:** 56

## Ingredient List:

- ½ a bowl of diced back bacon
- 2 large sized potatoes, peeled and cubed
- 400 grams of chopped tomatoes
- 8 ounces of chicken stock
- Salt and pepper
- 150 grams of dark green cabbage leaves, thinly sliced

||||||||||||||||||||||||||||||||||||||||||||||||||||||||||||||||||||||||||||

## Instructions:

1. Place the bacon into a large saucepan and cook over a medium temperature until the bacon turns brown all over.
2. Add the tomatoes, potatoes and chicken stock, add salt and pepper for seasoning. Bring the ingredients to a boil, turn the temperature down and allow it to simmer for 20 minutes.
3. Add the cabbage, and allow the ingredients to simmer for another 5 minutes.
4. Spoon the soup into bowls and serve.

# (13) Ham and Cabbage Soup

Barley, ham, onion, carrots, celery and cabbage all cooked in chicken broth to make a hearty healthy cabbage soup.

**Prep Time:** 20 **minutes**

**Total Prep Time:** 1 **hour** 30 **minutes**

**Yield:** 6 **people**

**Total Calories:** 55

**Ingredient List:**

- 825 milliliters of chicken stock
- 4 sticks of chopped celery
- 6 chopped carrots
- 1 chopped onion
- 2 cloves of finely chopped garlic
- 1 cabbage head, medium sized finely sliced
- 100 grams of pearl barley
- 225 grams of diced ham
- 2 Tbsp. of dried parsley

|||||||||||||||||||||||||||||||||||||||||||||||||||||||||||||||||||||||||

**Instructions:**

1. Place all of the ingredients into a large saucepan and bring to a boil over high heat.
2. Reduce the temperature to low and simmer for 1½ hours.

# (14) Cabbage, Carrot and Potato Soup

Cabbage, onion, potatoes and carrots are simmered together and then blended to make a simple but delicious vegetable soup. This makes a hearty lunch or dinner served with a crusty roll and sour cream.

**Prep Time:** 30 **minutes**

**Cook time:** 25 **minutes**

**Yield:** 6 **people**

**Total Calories:** 44

## Ingredient List:

- 4 thinly sliced large carrots
- 2 thinly sliced large potatoes
- 1 thinly sliced large onion
- ¼ thinly sliced cabbage, medium head
- 2 cloves of crushed garlic
- 1½ liters of chicken stock
- 1 Tbsp. of olive oil
- ¼ tsp. of dried thyme
- ¼ tsp. of dried basil
- 1 tsp. of dried parsley
- 1 tsp. of salt
- Ground black pepper

||||||||||||||||||||||||||||||||||||||||||||||||||||||||||||||||||||||||||||

## Instructions:

1. Add all of the ingredients into a large pot and cook over a medium temperature for 20 minutes.
2. Transfer the ingredients into a food processor and blend in batches until the ingredients are smooth.
3. Spoon the soup into bowls and serve.

# (15) Cabbage and Tomato Soup

Celery, peppers, cabbage, tomatoes, onions and carrots all simmered together to form this hearty soup packed full of vegetables.

**Prep Time:** 20 **minutes**

**Total Prep Time:** 25 **minutes**

**Yield:** 15 **people**

**Total Calories:** 66

## Ingredient List:

- 5 chopped carrots
- 3 chopped onions
- 2 tins of tomatoes, whole plum and peeled with the liquid
- 1 large cabbage head, chopped
- 1 packet of onion cup soup mixture
- 1 tin of green beans, cut and drained
- 2 liters of tomato juice
- 2 diced green peppers
- 10 chopped sticks of celery
- 400 milliliters of beef stock

||||||||||||||||||||||||||||||||||||||||||||||||||||||||||||||||||||||||||||||

## Instructions:

1. Place all ingredients into a large saucepan. Add enough water to cover the vegetables and cook until they become tender.
2. Spoon the soup into bowls and serve.

# (16) Simple Cabbage Soup

Made out of cabbage, carrots and tomatoes this is a delicious filling soup for a cold winter day.

**Prep Time:** 20 **minutes**

**Total Prep Time:** 3 **hours** 40 **minutes/ Yield:** 5 **people**

**Total Calories:** 39

**Ingredient List:**

- ½ a medium white cabbage head, chopped
- 4 diced large carrots
- 4 diced stalks of celery
- 1 minced onion
- 6 ounces of ketchup
- 12 ounces of tomato juice
- 1¼ pints of chicken stock
- 1 tin of chopped tomatoes

IIIIIIIIIIIIIIIIIIIIIIIIIIIIIIIIIIIIIIIIIIIIIIIIIIIIIIIIIIIIIIIIIIIIIIIIII

**Instructions:**

1. Place the carrots into a microwavable bowl and add 2 Tbsp. of water. Cook on high for 6 minutes.

2. Place the celery into a microwavable bowl, add 2 Tbsp. of water. Cook on high for 4 minutes.

3. Place the cabbage, carrots, celery, tomatoes and onions and chicken stock into a large saucepan. Cover and bring the ingredients to a boil for 30 minutes.

4. Turn the heat down and allow the ingredients to simmer for 3 hours.

5. Spoon the soup into bowls and serve.

# (17) Slow Cooker Cabbage and Cannellini Bean Soup

A hearty economical and healthy slow cooker cabbage soup recipe made with cannellini beans.

**Prep Time:** 15 **minutes**

**Total Prep Time:** 4 **hours**

**Yield:** 6 **people**

**Total Calories:**  37

**Ingredient List:**

- 1½ liters of vegetable stock
- 1 bay leaf
- 4 Tbsp. of dry white wine
- 2 tsp. of fresh rosemary, chopped
- 2 tsp. of fresh thyme, chopped
- 1 chopped onion
- 1 small shredded cabbage
- 2 tins of cannellini beans
- Salt and pepper

||||||||||||||||||||||||||||||||||||||||||||||||||||||||||||||||||||||||

**Instructions:**

3. Add all of the ingredients into a slow cooker and cook for 4 hours on high.

# (18) Beef Cabbage Soup

The main ingredients in the soup include onions, kidney beans, cabbage and minced beef. A very yummy dish that has been a favorite for many years.

**Prep Time:** 20 **minutes**

**Total Prep Time:** 6-8 **hours**

**Yield:** 10 **people**

**Total Calories:** 75

**Ingredient List:**

- 2 Tbsp. of vegetable oil
- 450 grams of minced beef
- ½ a chopped large onion
- 350 grams of chopped cabbage
- 500 milliliters of water
- 1 jar of passata
- 4 cubes of beef stock
- 1½ tsp. of ground cumin
- 1 tsp. of salt
- 1 tsp. of pepper

|||||||||||||||||||||||||||||||||||||||||||||||||||||||||||||||||||||||||||

**Instructions:**

1. In a large saucepan heat the oil over medium heat.

2. Add the onion and mince and cook until the beef is well browned. Drain the fat and place the beef into a slow cooker.

3. Add the water, passata, stock cubes, kidney beans, cabbage, salt and pepper into the slowcooker. Stir the ingredients to combine.

4. Cover the slow cooker and cook for 6 to 8 hours on a low setting making sure to stir the ingredients occasionally.

5. When cooked, spoon into bowls and serve.

# (19) Winter Spicy Cabbage Soup

A low fat healthy soup made from potatoes, shredded cabbage and butter beans.

**Prep Time:** 10 **minutes**

**Total Prep Time:** 30 **minutes**

**Yield:** 6 **people**

**Total Calories:** 43

**Ingredient List:**

- 1 Tbsp. of vegetable oil
- 1 chopped onion
- 1 shredded green cabbage
- 1 peeled large potato cut into cubes
- 1 tsp. of chilli powder or flakes
- 1 tsp. of ground coriander
- 1 tsp. of ground cumin
- 1 tsp. of ground fenugreek
- 1 liter of vegetable stock
- 1 tin of butter beans washed and drained
- Salt and pepper
- Crème fraiche

|||||||||||||||||||||||||||||||||||||||||||||||||||||||||||||||||||||||||||||||||

**Instructions:**

1. Heat the oil in a large saucepan over medium heat.

2. Fry the onions for 5 minutes.

3. Add the potatoes, shredded cabbage, stock and spices and bring it to a boil and then allow the ingredients to simmer for 15 minutes.

4. Pour in the butter beans and allow them to simmer for another 5 minutes.

5. Once the ingredients have softened up, transfer the soup into a food processor and blend.

6. Season with salt and pepper.

7. Spoon the soup into bowls, add the crème fraiche and serve.

# (20) Russian Cabbage Soup

This is a delicious European recipe made out of cabbage, carrot, tomatoes and celery. It's Cheap and quick and easy to make, and great for those winter evenings.

**Prep Time:** 20 **minutes**

**Total Prep Time:** 60 **minutes**

**Yield:** 8 **people**

**Total Calories:** 58

**Ingredient List:**

- 225 grams of thinly sliced tomatoes
- 140 grams of thinly sliced beetroot
- 1 liter of vegetable stock
- 2 Tbsp. of butter
- 250 grams of chopped onions
- 1 tsp. of caraway seed
- 2 tsp. of salt
- 1 chopped celery stick
- 1 large sliced carrot
- 250 grams of red cabbage coarsely chopped
- Black pepper
- ¼ tsp. of fresh dill
- 1 Tbsp. of cider vinegar
- 1 Tbsp. of honey
- 250 milliliters of passata
- Soured cream
- Chopped tomatoes

|||||||||||||||||||||||||||||||||||||||||||||||||||||||||||||||||||||||||||

**Instructions:**

1. Place the beetroot and the sliced potatoes in a large saucepan, cover with the vegetable stock and boil until the vegetables are cooked. Remove the beetroot and the potatoes with a slotted spoon and keep the stock.

2. In a large frying pan heat the butter over medium heat. Add the caraway seeds, onions and salt, cook until the onions become translucent and soft. Add the cabbage, carrots and celery. Add the stock that you put to one side, cover and cook for approximately 10 minutes.

3. Add the beetroot and the potatoes, season with the dill and the black pepper. Add the passata, honey, and cider vinegar. Put a lid on the saucepan, turn the heat down to medium, and allow it to simmer for at least 30 minutes.

4. Spoon the soup into bowls, garnish with the sour cream, fresh tomatoes and dill.

# Chapter III - Assortment of Cabbage Recipes

||||||||||||||||||||||||||||||||||||||||||||||||||||||||||||||||||||||||||||||||||||||

# (21) Cabbage Pancakes

A deliciously unique way to serve pancakes. Sautéed cabbage is combined with pancake batter to make the perfect side dish or snack.

**Prep Time:** 15 **minutes**

**Total Prep Time:** 30 **minutes**

**Yield:** 15 **people**

**Total Calories:** 56

## Ingredient List:

- 1 Tbsp. of olive oil
- ½ a small head of cabbage, thinly sliced and cored
- 1 thinly sliced onion
- Black pepper
- 150 milliliters of milk
- 4 Tbsp. of vegetable oil
- 2 large eggs
- 250 grams of plain flour
- 4 tsp. of baking powder
- 1 tsp. of bicarbonate of soda
- 1 tsp. of butter

|||||||||||||||||||||||||||||||||||||||||||||||||||||||||||||||||||||||||||

**Instructions:**

1.  In a large frying pan heat the olive oil over medium heat. Add the onion and the cabbage and cook for 10 minutes. Season with pepper and set the pan to one side to cool down.

2.  In a large bowl, whisk together the eggs, vegetable oil, milk and yogurt.

3.  In a separate large bowl combine the bicarbonate of soda, baking powder, and flour. Make a hole in the middle of the dry ingredients, pour in the wet ingredients and stir to combine.

4.  Add the onions and cabbage to the batter and stir to combine.

5.  Over medium, heat a large frying pan and cook the pancake mix in batches.

6.  Divide onto plates and serve.

# (22) Cabbage and Onion Mixture

A delicious but simple stew made from mushrooms, onions, cabbage and chicken stock.

**Prep Time:** 10 minutes

**Total Prep Time:** 35 minutes

**Yield:** 3 people

**Total Calories:** 45

**Ingredient List:**

- ½ a chopped celery stalk
- 1 chopped onion
- ½ a chopped carrot
- 1 tsp. of grated ginger
- ½ a tsp. of minced garlic
- 3 cups of cabbage
- 2 Tbsp. of chicken stock
- 3 tsp. of beef granules
- 1 cup of chopped mushrooms
- 2 cups of water
- 1 cup of chopped baby mushrooms
- 1 Tbsp. of chopped chives

||||||||||||||||||||||||||||||||||||||||||||||||||||||||||||||||||||||||||||

**Instructions:**

1. In a large saucepan add the mushrooms, celery, garlic, ginger, onion, carrot and cabbage, add the chicken stock, stir to come and bring the ingredients to a boil for 20 minutes.

2. Add the beef granules and the water. Put a lid over the saucepan and allow it to cook for another 15 minutes.

3. Spoon the stew into bowls, garnish with the chives and serve.

# (23) Barbecued Cabbage

Chunks of cabbage doused in seasoning and butter, this recipe makes a delicious side dish for any meal.

**Prep Time:** 10 **minutes**

**Total Prep Time:** 30 **minutes**

**Yield:** 8 **people**

**Total Calories:** 45

## Ingredient List:

- 1 large cabbage head cored and sliced into 8 pieces.
- 8 Tbsp. of softened butter.
- 4 Tbsp. of water.
- ½ a tsp. of garlic granules
- ½ a tsp. of seasoned salt
- Ground black pepper

||||||||||||||||||||||||||||||||||||||||||||||||||||||||||||||||||||||||||||||||

## Instructions:

1. Preheat the barbeque on a medium to high temperature and oil the grate.
2. Place the cabbage wedges into a large baking dish.
3. Add the water into the baking dish.
4. Put a tsp. of butter on top of each cabbage wedge.
5. Season with the garlic granules and the salt and pepper.
6. Place foil over the dish and put it onto the barbeque.
7. Cook for approximately 30 minutes until the cabbage becomes tender.
8. Once cooked, divide onto dishes and serve.

# (24) Cabbage Tofu Noodles Mix

A tasty healthy and filling meal made with chicken, cabbage, noodles, carrots and tofu.

**Prep Time:** 10 **minutes**

**Total Prep Time:** 60 **minutes**

**Yield:** 3 **people**

**Total Calories:** 67

**Ingredient List:**

- ¼ pound of chicken
- 2 diced carrots
- ⅓ cup of soy sauce
- ½ a tsp. of white sugar
- Salt
- 3 cups of cabbage
- 2 packs of cubed noodles
- 1 packet of noodles
- 2 diced leeks

||||||||||||||||||||||||||||||||||||||||||||||||||||||||||||||||||||||||||||

## Instructions:

1. Place the cabbage, chicken, carrots, salt and sugar into a large saucepan. Cover the ingredients and allow them to cook for 10 minutes on a medium heat.

2. Add the mushrooms, soy sauce, and tofu and stir to combine and allow it to continue cooking.

3. Cook the noodles according to the directions on the packet.

4. Drain the noodles and add them to the cabbage mix, add the leaks and allow the ingredients to continue cooking for 30 minutes.

5. Spoon the meal into bowls and serve.

# (25) Braised Cabbage

This cabbage recipe is simply irresistible. Braised with chicken stock and butter until sweet and tender it makes an ideal side dish for any meal.

**Prep Time:** 5 **minutes**

**Total Prep Time:** 45 **minutes**

**Yield:** 6 **people**

**Total Calories:** 48

**Ingredient List:**

- 2 tsp. of butter
- 425 milliliters of chicken stock
- 1 cabbage head, cored and chopped coarsely
- Salt and pepper

|||||||||||||||||||||||||||||||||||||||||||||||||||||||||||||||||||||||||||||||

**Instructions:**

1. In a large frying pan add the chicken stock and the butter and bring it to a boil. Turn the heat down and add the cabbage.
2. Put a lid over the ingredients and cook on a low temperature for 45 minutes. Season with salt and pepper.
3. Divide onto plates and serve.

# (26) Beef, Cabbage and Mushroom Noodles

A satisfying meal made from cabbage, beef, onions, celery and mushrooms.

**Prep Time:** 10 **minutes**

**Total Prep Time:** 50 **minutes**

**Yield:** 2 **people**

**Total Calories:** 74

**Ingredient List:**

- ¾ cups of soy sauce
- 3 cups of cabbage
- ¼ cup of white sugar
- 8 ounces of noodles
- 2 Tbsp. of canola oil
- 1 pound of sliced sirloin beef
- 1 sliced onion
- 1 Tbsp. of canola oil
- 2 sliced stalks of celery
- 2 sliced carrots
- 5 pieces of green onions
- 4 mushrooms, sliced

**Instructions:**

1. Put the cabbage, sugar and soy sauce into a large bowl and mix together thoroughly.

2. Boil the noodles according to the instructions on the packet. Once the noodles are cooked, set them to one side.

3. Heat the canola oil in a frying pan over a medium temperature and cook the beef until it becomes tender. This should take approximately 10 minutes.

4. Add the onions, carrots, mushrooms and celery to the beef and stir to combine.

5. Add the noodles and the green onions to the beef mixture and allow the ingredients to simmer for 25 minutes.

6. Spoon into bowls and serve.

# (27) Potato and Cabbage Sauté

This Ethiopian dish is simple yet delicious, made with potatoes, carrots, cabbage and onions sautéed in turmeric and cumin.

**Prep Time:** 25 **minutes**

**Total Prep Time:** 60 **minutes**

**Yield:** 6 **people**

**Total Calories:** 64)

## Ingredient List:

- 120 milliliters of olive oil
- 4 thinly sliced carrots
- 1 thinly sliced onion
- 1 tsp. of salt
- ½ a tsp. of ground black pepper
- ½ a tsp. of ground cumin
- ¼ tsp. of ground turmeric
- ½ a head of finely chopped cabbage
- 5 peeled and cubed potatoes

llllllllllllllllllllllllllllllllllllllllllllllllllllllllllllllllllllll

## Instructions:

1. Heat the olive oil in a large frying pan on the medium heat.
2. Cook the onions and the carrots for approximately 5 minutes.
3. Add the cabbage, turmeric, salt and pepper, stir to combine and cook for 20 minutes.
4. Add the potatoes cubes, put a lid over the ingredients, turn the heat down to low and cook for more 30 minutes.
5. Divide onto plates and serve.

# (28) Vegetable Noodles

A healthy noodle dish packed with an assortment of vegetables.

**Prep Time:** 10 **minutes**

**Total Prep Time:** 50 **minutes**

**Yield:** 2 **people**

**Total Calories:** 54

## Ingredient List:

- 2 packets of noodles
- 4 Tbsp. of soy sauce
- 4 Tbsp. of sesame oil
- 1 Tbsp. of rice vinegar
- 1 Tbsp. of caster sugar
- ½ a Tbsp. of chilli oil
- 3 cups of cabbage
- 1 pinch of red pepper
- 1 bunch of spring onions, sliced
- 2 carrots, sliced

|||||||||||||||||||||||||||||||||||||||||||||||||||||||||||||||||||||||||||

**Instructions:**

1. Boil the noodles in a large pot according to the directions on the packet. When cooked, rinse them in cold water and set them to one side.

2. Place the cabbage, sugar, chilli oil, sesame oil, vinegar and soy sauce into a bowl. Stir together thoroughly.

3. Add the noodles into the cabbage mixture and toss to coat them with the mixture.

4. Place all the ingredients into a large frying pan and cook for approximately 30 minutes.

5. Divide into bowls and serve.

# (29) Pork Oriental Cabbage Rolls

Minced pork combined with crunchy water chestnuts, fresh ginger and soy sauce to make this highly flavored Oriental style cabbage roll.

**Prep Time:** 10 **minutes**

**Total Prep Time:** 30 **minutes**

**Yield:** 4 **people**

**Total Calories:** 75

**Ingredient List:**

- 500 grams of minced pork, extra lean
- 1 can of water chestnuts, finely chopped and drained
- 2 Tbsp. of five-spice powder
- 1 Tbsp. of fresh root ginger finely grated
- 2 finely chopped spring onions
- 2 Tbsp. of dark soy sauce
- 2 cloves of crushed garlic
- 1 beaten egg
- 8 large cabbage leaves
- 450 milliliters of chicken stock
- 2 tsp. of corn flour
- 1 tsp. of sweet chilli sauce
- Spring onion for garnish

IIIIIIIIIIIIIIIIIIIIIIIIIIIIIIIIIIIIIIIIIIIIIIIIIIIIIIIIIIIIIIIIIIIIIIIIIIIIII

**Instructions:**

1. In a large bowl, place the egg, garlic, soy sauce, spring onions, ginger, five spice powder, and water chestnuts. Use your hands to combine the ingredients together thoroughly and then divide it into 8 portions.

2. Cut the stalk out of the cabbage and spoon the pork mixture into the center of each cabbage leaf. Wrap the leaf up to enclose the filling.

3. Pour the stock into a steamer and add the cabbage rolls into the steamer with the joint side facing downwards. Allow the cabbage rolls to steam for 15 minutes.

4. In a small bowl combine the corn flour with water and stir to combine. Add it to the stock at the bottom of the steamer. Bring it to a boil until it gets slightly thick.

5. Add the chilli sauce to the stock mixture and stir to combine.

6. Place the cabbage rolls onto plates, spoon the sauce over the top and garnish with the spring onions.

# (30) Stuffed Cabbage Rolls

This is a famous Russian dish of precooked cabbage leaves stuffed with a rice and a mince filling.

**Prep Time:** 10 **minutes**

**Total Prep Time:** 2 **hours**

**Yield:** 8 **people**

**Total Calories:** 87

**Ingredient List:**

- 1 cabbage
- 140 grams of rice
- 3 Tbsp. of oil
- 2 chopped onions
- 500 grams of minced beef
- 300 grams of minced pork
- Salt and pepper
- 3 grated carrots
- 3 Tbsp. of tomato puree
- 2 Tbsp. of soured cream
- 225 milliliters of water

||||||||||||||||||||||||||||||||||||||||||||||||||||||||||||||||||||||||||

**Instructions:**

1. Cut out the core of the cabbage.

2. Fill a large sized saucepan ⅓ of the way with water and let it boil.

3. Add the cabbage and cook for 20 minutes. When cooked, drain and allow the cabbage to cool down before cutting off the leaves, one at a time.

4. Cook the rice according to the directions on the packet.

5. Heat 2 Tbsp. of oil in a frying pan then cook one of the onions.

6. In a large bowl add the rice, mince, cooked onions, salt and pepper and combine together thoroughly using your hands.

7. Spoon a Tbsp. of meat filling onto the end of the cabbage leaf, fold and then roll. Repeat the same process with the rest of the cabbage.

8. Heat the rest of the oil in a frying pan and fry the cabbage rolls for a few minutes on each side.

9. In a small bowl combine the tomato puree with the sour cream, add some water and salt and whisk to combine.

10. Transfer the cabbage rolls into a casserole dish, sprinkle with carrots and onions and then pour the sauce over the top.

11. Put a lid over the cabbage rolls and cook over a medium heat for 45 minutes.

# About the Author

Nancy Silverman is an accomplished chef from Essex, Vermont. Armed with her degree in Nutrition and Food Sciences from the University of Vermont, Nancy has excelled at creating e-books that contain healthy and delicious meals that anyone can make and everyone can enjoy. She improved her cooking skills at the New England Culinary Institute in Montpelier Vermont and she has been working at perfecting her culinary style since graduation. She claims that her life's work is always a work in progress and she only hopes to be an inspiration to aspiring chefs everywhere.

Her greatest joy is cooking in her modern kitchen with her family and creating inspiring and delicious meals. She often says that she has perfected her signature dishes based on her family's critique of each and every one.

Nancy has her own catering company and has also been fortunate enough to be head chef at some of Vermont's most exclusive restaurants. When a friend suggested she share some of her outstanding signature dishes, she decided to add cookbook author to her repertoire of personal achievements. Being a technological savvy woman, she felt the e-book realm would be a better fit and soon she had her first cookbook available online. As of today, Nancy has sold over 1,000 e-books and has shared her culinary experiences and brilliant recipes with people from all over the world! She plans on expanding into self-help books and dietary cookbooks, so stayed tuned!

# Author's Afterthoughts

Thank you for making the decision to invest in one of my cookbooks! I cherish all my readers and hope you find joy in preparing these meals as I have.

There are so many books available and I am truly grateful that you decided to buy this one and follow it from beginning to end.

I love hearing from my readers on what they thought of this book and any value they received from reading it. As a personal favor, I would appreciate any feedback you can give in the form of a review on Amazon and please be honest! This kind of support will help others make an informed choice on and will help me tremendously in producing the best quality books possible.

My most heartfelt thanks,

*Nancy Silverman*

*If you're interested in more of my books, be sure to follow my author page on Amazon (can be found on the link Bellow) or scan the QR-Code.*

*https://www.amazon.com/author/nancy-silverman*

Made in the
USA
Monee, IL